For Jayman —D.R.

Thank you to Esther Cajahuaringa, Rotem Moscovich,
Karen Smith, and Marietta Zacker for invaluable contributions.

For Easton and Elliot —M.T.

THIS IS A BORZOI BOOK PUBLISHED BY ALFRED A. KNOPF

Text copyright © 2024 by Dean Robbins
Jacket art and interior illustrations copyright © 2024 by Matt Tavares

All rights reserved. Published in the United States by Alfred A. Knopf, an imprint of Random House Children's Books,
a division of Penguin Random House LLC, New York.

Knopf, Borzoi Books, and the colophon are registered trademarks of Penguin Random House LLC.

Visit us on the Web! rhcbooks.com
Educators and librarians, for a variety of teaching tools, visit us at RHTeachersLibrarians.com

Library of Congress Cataloging-in-Publication Data is available upon request.
ISBN 978-0-593-47925-4 (trade) — ISBN 978-0-593-47926-1 (lib. bdg.) — ISBN 978-0-593-47927-8 (ebook)

The text of this book is set in 16-point Amasis.
The illustrations were created digitally.

Editors: Karen Smith and Esther Cajahuaringa • Copy Editor: Artie Bennett
Designer: Sarah Hokanson • Production Manager: Melissa Fariello
Managing Editor: Jake Eldred • Production Manager: Melissa Fariello

MANUFACTURED IN CHINA   10 9 8 7 6 5 4 3 2 1   First Edition

The SHAPE of THINGS

HOW MAPMAKERS PICTURE OUR WORLD

Words by
DEAN ROBBINS

Pictures by
MATT TAVARES

Alfred A. Knopf  New York

Mountains rose in the east.
A lake shimmered in the west.
A valley stretched out far below.

Where did the creek flow?
Where did the trails lead?
Where did the woods end?

Mother drew dots on a cave wall.

Father etched grooves into a mammoth tusk.

Children sketched spirals in the sand.

These were some of Earth's first maps.
Pictures of where things are.
And a guide to the world around us.

Native Americans created maps with rocks.
One showed the rivers of the Shoshone-Bannock homeland.

Egyptians created maps with papyrus.
One showed trees, a temple, and a well.

In ancient Babylonia, an artist looked up, down, left, and right.

A wide space lay before him.

He carved what he saw on a clay tablet.

The path from rivers . . .

to cities . . .

to hills.

His map helped others make sense of the unique landscape.

The Greeks wondered about the shape of the whole world.
Some thought it was a rectangle.

Some thought it was a cylinder.

Some thought it was a flat disk with monsters beyond the edges.

And some thought it was a sphere.

The Chinese created maps with wood.
One showed the forests and canyons of the Qin Kingdom.

Polynesians created maps with shells and sticks.
One showed wave patterns around an island.

Much later, European explorers traveled by land and sea to chart our planet.
They went south, north, and west and proved that it was round.

How did the parts of this round Earth connect to each other? A German sailor tried to fit them all together on a papier-mâché globe.

More and more, people wanted
to get from country to country.

From continent to continent.

So they invented a new way of making maps
that mixed art and science.

First, surveyors measured the shape of things
with special tools.

A compass to find directions.

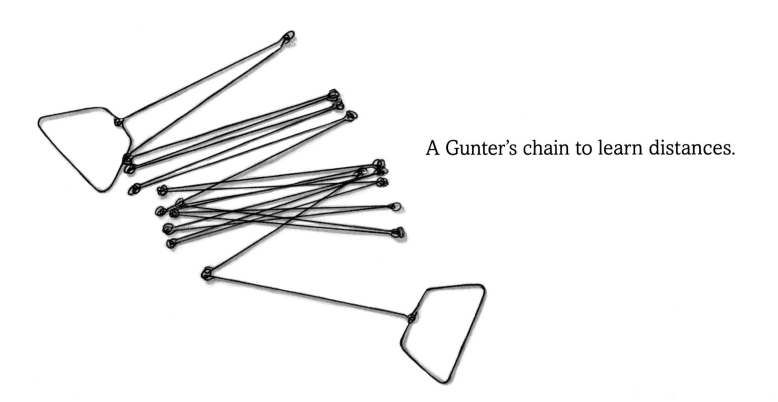

A Gunter's chain to learn distances.

A theodolite to check the angles.

With those measurements, they used geometry to figure the length between fields and forests. And to mark the size of meadows and oceans.

Next, cartographers turned these
calculations into pictures.
They drew . . .
and shaded . . .

and colored . . .
so all people could understand the world around them.

Mountains rise in the east.
A lake shimmers in the west.
A valley stretches out far below.

Today, surveyors measure our landscape with electronic tools, like satellites and lasers.

Then cartographers use computers to draw . . .

and shade . . .

and color . . .

so we can understand the world around us.

The world we all share.

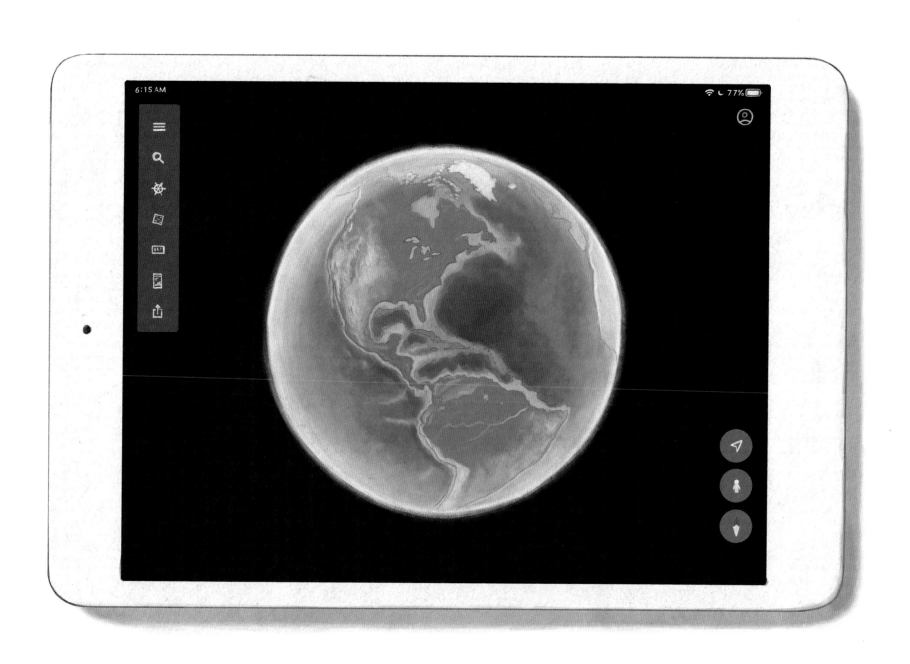

Timeline

25,000 BCE: One of the world's oldest maps, engraved on a mammoth tusk - - - - - - - ➤ **10,000 BCE:** Map of the Snake River Valley, carved on a boulder in present-day Idaho by the Shoshone-Bannock tribe - - - - - - - - - -

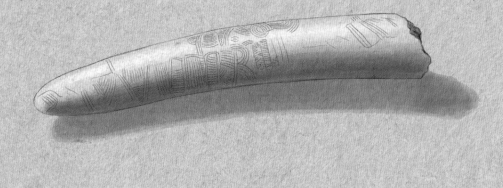

800 BCE: Greek map of the Earth as a flat disk, imagined by Homer - - - - - - - ➤ **600 BCE:** Babylonian map of the Earth, engraved on a clay tablet - - - - - - - - -

1200 BCE: Egyptian map of Wadi Hammamat, drawn on papyrus

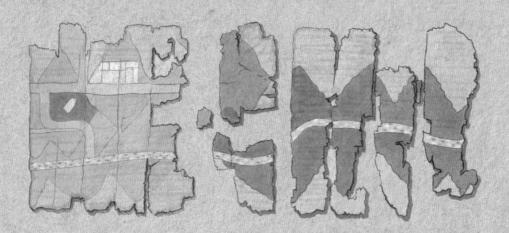

500 BCE: Greek map of the Earth as a rectangle, imagined by Anaximenes of Miletus

500 BCE: Greek map of the Earth as a cylinder, imagined by Anaximander

300 BCE: Greek map of the Earth as a sphere, imagined by Aristotle

200 BCE: Chinese map of the Qin Kingdom, drawn on wood

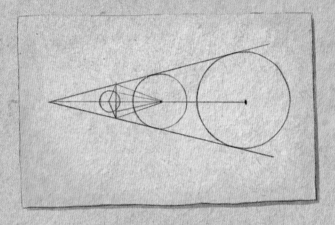

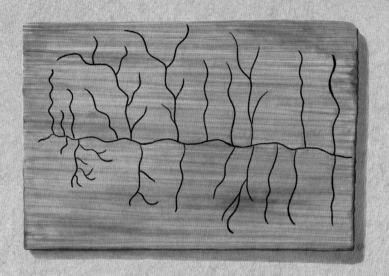

1600: Map based on measurements taken with a compass, Gunter's chain, and theodolite

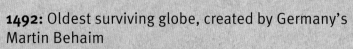

200 BCE: Polynesian stick chart, representing ocean currents

1492: Oldest surviving globe, created by Germany's Martin Behaim

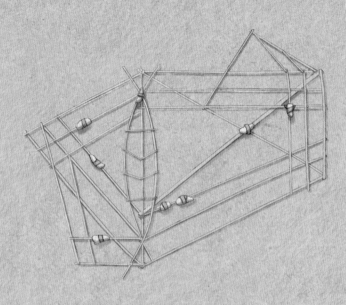

2000: Map created by a satellite orbiting the Earth

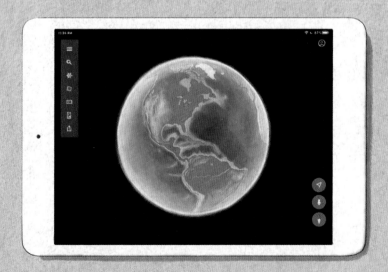

Author's Note

A map is a picture that shows where things are and how they connect to each other. Maps can help you see the whole world—or different parts of it—on a piece of paper, a globe, or a computer screen. They include mountains, oceans, rivers, roads, and lots more.

No one knows exactly who made the earliest surviving maps, which are cave paintings and bone carvings from 17,000 to 27,000 years ago. The practice of taking measurements to create maps existed in ancient civilizations at least 5,000 years ago.

Cultures made different kinds of maps based on their observations of the world. They used materials available to them, including rocks, bark, shells, wood, sticks, papyrus, and clay. In the 1400s, German mapmaker Martin Behaim (1459–1507) fashioned the oldest surviving globe out of papier-mâché.

Modern surveying and cartography began in the 1500s with special tools for measuring the land. In the United States, presidents George Washington (1732–1799), Thomas Jefferson (1743–1826), Abraham Lincoln (1809–1865), and Theodore Roosevelt (1858–1919) all worked as mapmakers. Benjamin Banneker (1731–1806) was a celebrated surveyor who helped mark the boundaries of Washington, D.C., in 1791.

Men and women of all backgrounds work as surveyors and cartographers. Anyone can learn the job, including you! Study hard in math, science, and art, and you too can make beautiful maps that help people understand the world around them.

Illustrator's Note

Before I started working on this book, I had never thought much about maps. But as I immersed myself in the research, I became fascinated with the subject. I started thinking about all the ways that maps have changed, even during my lifetime. When I was a kid, back when there were no smartphones and no internet (if you can believe that), family road trips usually involved picking up a free map at a gas station. From the passenger seat, one of us would unfold the giant paper map and navigate.

Maps have changed quite a bit since then! With modern digital maps, we can type in an address and zoom in to just about any spot on the planet. Now when we go on road trips, we all have maps built into our phones or into our car's GPS navigation system. Our maps update in real time to help guide us toward our destination.

It was amazing to learn how far maps have come over the years, and I can't wait to see what new innovations will emerge from the next generation of mapmakers.

Mapmaking Tricks and Tools

Surveyors measure the land, while cartographers use their measurements to make maps.

Surveying is needed to create roads, bridges, or buildings. Human beings have been doing it ever since they began making large structures thousands of years ago.

Surveyors and cartographers know a lot about math, especially a kind of math called geometry. Geometry explores circles, squares, and other shapes. It helps cartographers produce maps with the measurements they receive from surveyors.

Hundreds of years ago, surveyors took measurements with chains, compasses, and marking pins. Today's surveyors have fancier electronic tools, including computers, lasers, and robots. They can also do their work in the sky, using airplanes, helicopters, or drones to measure large parts of the Earth that aren't easy to reach by land.

Here are some of the tools surveyors and cartographers use in our day.

- An **electronic theodolite** measures horizontal and vertical angles.
- An **automatic level** is a kind of telescope that measures the height of objects in the distance.
- A **magnetic locator** helps find metal objects underground.
- A **3-D scanner** attaches to the bottom of an aircraft to take perfect pictures of the land.
- The **Global Positioning System,** or GPS, uses signals from satellites in outer space to measure locations on Earth. Surveyors use GPS receivers to take accurate measurements in an instant.

What Mapmakers Love

- **Art** allows people to create drawings, paintings, sculpture, and other beautiful objects using their imaginations.
- **Math,** or mathematics, is a science that explains numbers and shapes.
- **Science** is a way to understand how the world works by doing experiments. Experiments are tests that help scientists learn new things.
- **Astronomy** is a science that looks beyond Earth's atmosphere to the sun, the moon, the planets, and the stars.
- **Engineering** is a way to make things by using math and science. Engineers are problem solvers who build structures, work with electrical power, or design machines.
- **Geography** is a science that explores the Earth's surface, from oceans to mountains to deserts.
- **Geometry** is a kind of math that works with lines, circles, squares, and other shapes.
- **Physics** is a science that shows how everything in the universe behaves, from the smallest atoms to the largest stars.
- **Trigonometry** is a kind of math that studies angles and triangles.

Bibliography

Brocklehurst, Ruth; illustrated by Linda Edwards. *Children's Picture Atlas*. London: Usborne Publishing, 2004.

Cerami, Charles A., and Robert M. Silverstein. *Benjamin Banneker: Surveyor, Astronomer, Publisher, Patriot*. Hoboken, NJ: John Wiley & Sons, 2002.

Harley, J. B., and David Woodward, editors. *The History of Cartography*. Chicago: University of Chicago Press, 1987.

Mizielinska, Aleksandra, and Daniel Mizielinski. *Maps*. London: Big Picture Press, 2013.

Nathanson, Jerry A., Michael T. Lanzafama, and Philip Kissam. *Surveying Fundamentals and Practices*. New York: Pearson, 2017.

Short, John. *The World Through Maps: A History of Cartography*. Richmond Hill, Ontario, Canada: Firefly Books, 2003.